Cracking

Shôn Dale-Jones

methuen | drama

LONDON • NEW YORK • OXFORD • NEW DELHI • SYDNEY

METHUEN DRAMA
Bloomsbury Publishing Plc
50 Bedford Square, London, WC1B 3DP, UK
1385 Broadway, New York, NY 10018, USA
29 Earlsfort Terrace, Dublin 2, Ireland

BLOOMSBURY, METHUEN DRAMA and the Methuen
Drama logo are trademarks of Bloomsbury Publishing Plc

First published in Great Britain 2024

A catalogue record for this book is available from the British Library.

A catalog record for this book is available from the Library of Congress.

ISBN: PB: 978-1-3504-7695-0
ePDF: 978-1-3504-7696-7
eBook: 978-1-3504-7697-4

Series: Modern Plays

Typeset by Mark Heslington Ltd, Scarborough, North Yorkshire

To find out more about our authors and books visit
www.bloomsbury.com and sign up for our newsletters.

Cracking was originally commissioned by BBC Radio 4 as a one-off drama, produced by BBC Audio Drama Wales in Cardiff. It was broadcast on 17 August 2023 before being made available on BBC Sounds.

The first live performance of *Cracking* was presented by SDJ Productions, co-produced by Theatre Royal Plymouth, at Theatr Clwyd on 11 October 2023 before touring nationally and internationally.

Writer/Performer	Shôn Dale-Jones
Original Music	John Biddle
Directed by	Helena Middleton
In collaboration with	Stefanie Mueller, Alex Byrne, Dom Coyote, John Norton
Marketing	Justine Watkins-Fife
Graphic Design	Claire O'Neill
Website	Wes Fife

Cracking is inspired by real life events – a gang of internet trolls turned up on Shôn's doorstep, aggressively accusing him and his wife of doing something they hadn't done.

For a moment, life spun and turned upside down as all hell was let loose.

This play was written with the hope that hatred will be overcome by the beauty of this world.

Thanks to

John Nicholson, Elizabet Topp, Josie Dale-Jones, David Pagan, Julian Spooner, Jon Ferguson, Simon Stokes for reading and feeding back on drafts of the script.

All the people I've ever collaborated with. Although this show is a one-person show, I've been inspired and supported by many brilliant artists along the way – their support and encouragement, their skill and insight are fundamental to the making process.

All the wonderful friends who supported us through this very strange time, holding our hands through the darkness, keeping us steady and filling us with love.

Special thanks to Stefanie Mueller. She has been my long-time collaborator, playing a huge part in everything I've ever made – as an editor, dramaturg, designer, director, you name it.

Shôn Dale-Jones

The publication of this new play coincides with thirty years of theatre-making. Shôn has been making theatre since 1994. Over the last thirty years he has created twenty-nine live shows and six BBC radio plays as well as several short films, a BBC TV pilot and site-specific work. He has been translated into seven languages (Brazilian/Portuguese, Norwegian, Turkish, Russian, German, French and Flemish) toured to over 200 UK venues, played at nine London theatres and presented work across twenty countries on six continents, including the Meyerhold Theatre, Moscow; Sydney Opera House; Barrow Street Theatre, New York; Harbourfront Centre, Toronto; Dublin Theatre Festival; National Museum, Singapore and the Walker Arts Center, Minneapolis. He has worked with the BBC, Barbican, Royal Court, National Theatre Studios and National Theatre Wales, winning various awards – including BBC Audio Award for Best Comedy Drama, two Fringe Firsts, a Total Theatre Award and a nomination for a Prix Europa for Best European Radio Fiction.

Up until the pandemic in 2020, Shôn made work as Artistic Director of Hoipolloi – an independent international touring company – and as Hugh Hughes, the emerging Welsh artist.

Between 2016 and 2019 Shôn created *The Loose Change Trilogy*. The three shows, *The Duke, Me & Robin Hood* and *The Ladder*, were written, produced and presented to raise money and awareness for refugees, street children and climate change. The shows were performed over 300 times around the world including at the Royal Court, Barbican, Adelaide International Festival and NonStop International Festival, Norway; translated into four languages; adapted for BBC Radio 4; and raised over £100,000 to support the work of Save The Children, Street Child United and World Wildlife Foundation.

Since 2020 he has worked as an independent artist. He made *Possible*, an online and on stage show for National Theatre Wales; *Your Call*, a radio show, as part of Arts Council England's *Culture In Quarantine* programme, with his daughter Josie Dale-Jones; *Still Floating*, a live solo storytelling show; wrote and directed *Straight Faced* for Bragteatret, Norway; co-created and toured *Every Word Was Once an Animal* with Belgian company Ontroerend Goed; collaborated with Zoë Svendsen and Metis on *Love Letters to a Liveable Future*, with Canadian theatre-maker, Adam Lazarus and poet/performer, Hannah Jane Walker.

Shôn is currently reviving *The Duke*, developing *Cracking* for the screen, creating a new multi-platformed show called *Stories From An Invisible Town* and working on a comedy about protestors and protesting.

To find out more, visit his website: sdjproductions.co.uk

Stage Shows and Radio Shows

2023   Cracking

2023   Cracking (for radio)

2022   Still Floating

2021   Straight Faced (for Brageteatret, Norway)

2021   Possible (for National Theatre Wales)

2021   Love Letters to a Liveable Future (with Metis)

2020   Your Call (for radio)

2020   Every Word Was Once an Animal (with Ontroerend Goed)

2019   Me & Robin Hood (for radio)

2019   The Ladder

2018   The Duke (for radio)

2018   Unconditional (collaboration with ThisEgg)

2017   Me & Robin Hood

2016   The Duke

2013   Things I Forgot I Remembered

2012   A Disappearing Town (for radio)

2012   Stories from an Invisible Town

2009   360

2009   Floating (for radio)

2008   The Doubtful Guest

2007   Story of a Rabbit

2006   The Impostor

2005   Floating

2004   Ablaze!

Review Quotes From Past Work

A legend of the Edinburgh Festival
The Stage

The great Welsh storyteller
StageDoor

Natural comic
The Guardian

A natural storyteller
The List

A mesmerising personality
The Guardian

It's impossible not to be drawn into the tales he weaves
British Theatre Guide

He makes the real world seem wondrous. You
won't find a show with a bigger, better heart
What's On Stage

Charming, surreal, warm-hearted
The Scotsman

Heartfelt and insightful stuff that has great power to move
Evening Standard

A poignancy that takes you by surprise
The Guardian

Full of underlying truths about what it is to be human
Telegraph

Should be prescribed as medicine for depressives
Metro

The hilarious stories are a joy to listen to
Telegraph

The most generous of hosts
The Guardian

Introduction to *Cracking*

I've enjoyed the greatest pleasure and the biggest privilege to make theatre for thirty years. I've met some wonderful people, worked with brilliant and inspiring artists and visited lots of fantastic places. Every project I've ever worked on has started from a different inspiration and found it's own form. Choosing what to work on has always been clear – a real need to make and share a story emerges and feels too difficult to ignore.

I wrote *Cracking* in response to real life events that happened on our doorstep in April 2022. My wife, Steffi, and I opened the door to find some real life internet trolls aggressively accusing us of something we hadn't done. However much we tried, there was no way of engaging them in a conversation. After managing to persuade them to get off our doorstep, they returned three more times over the next fortnight. On top of this, they dropped leaflets around our neighbourhood telling people we were potentially suspect characters that couldn't be trusted. The situation escalated and threatened to fall out of control. Feeling the fear of being threatened by an angry headless beast, I eventually turned to writing – to process the situation and share the story.

Since writing the radio drama and performing this stage play, I've been reminded that many people are decent, honest, warm-hearted and lovely. I've been reminded how many of us want to find a way of re-building our world. I've been reminded of the importance of standing up for what we believe in. I've been reminded of the need to connect to each other. I've been reminded that it takes effort to create communities.

All this to say, we have a fight on our hands, and that the fight is worth fighting, because this world can be beautiful.

Shôn Dale-Jones

Cracking

This play is dedicated to Josie Dale-Jones and other theatre-makers like her who have the courage to make work that encourages us to make this world feel like home to more of us

There will be many ways to stage this show. I'm sure it doesn't even need to be a one-person performance. If it inspires you to present the story in another form, please be my guest.

Originally, I wrote this piece for myself to perform. I saw this play as a straightforward piece of storytelling. When I performed it I had a desk, a chair and two microphones on stage. One microphone had various vocal effects, the other didn't. The microphones were not always used – sometimes I used my natural voice. (This script does not indicate when the microphones were used, but, as a general rule, I used the microphones to support the voice of the characters.) I used a general lighting wash throughout the show. There were no lighting changes. For me, this encouraged an emphasis on the telling of the story and the use of the audience's imagination. I wanted the images to lie in their minds, rather than on stage. I had a laptop and a vocoder on the desk. I operated sound and music through the laptop. In fact, I operated the whole show myself. I had two eggs on the desk, sitting in egg cups. And I had a wig which I wore for one section.

For a feeling of authenticity, I used my real name and wore my own everyday clothes. For the sake of this script, I have used my real name.

As the audience entered, I stood near the entrance, welcoming everyone into the theatre. Once everyone had arrived, I walked on stage.

Hello, my name is Shôn. Shôn is my real name – the name my mother gave me and the name I have used ever since

It's a really big pleasure to be here
And that is what I always say at the beginning of this show
Although tonight, being here with you, right now, saying it, feels right
It feels like I'd want to say it, even if I hadn't planned to
I'd want to say it, even if I hadn't planned to
Because it really is a big pleasure to be here

It's a really big pleasure being here

Obviously I'm not going to start the show saying
It's a big pain in the arse being here

Music.

I don't want to be here, I don't want to be here, I really don't
want to be here

Although, you know what, the truth is, I wish the events that
led me to being here hadn't happened, and so, in that way, I
wish I didn't have to be here

I wish I didn't have to be here

It's a really big pleasure being here

Thanks for coming

This show is called, *Cracking*

Music.

I can see some of you liked that more than others. It's to be
expected
I made that track all on my own

Let me explain how this show is going to work
I will be the only person on stage here tonight. No one else
will appear
I will be using these two microphones, this vocoder and this
laptop
This laptop has all the sound and music we need for the show
You'll see I covered up the logo, but it's obvious it's an
Apple Mac
I will operate the whole show on my own

Music.

Just having fun, joking around

Now, let's be serious

Over the course of the next hour or so, I will tell you a story
A story inspired by real life events
Real life events that happened last year

Real life events that I couldn't believe were happening
Real life events that were difficult and challenging
Real life events that made me wonder what sort of world are
we living in

I suppose what I've done is I've taken those real life events
and made a story out of them. You could say, I've taken
reality and turned it into fantasy
Which is something the great Spanish-Mexican filmmaker
Luis Buñuel has something to say about

Music.

*Fantasy and reality are equally personal and equally felt and so their
difference is a matter of only relative importance*

In case some of you didn't quite catch that . . .

Fantasy and reality are equally personal and equally felt and
so their difference is a matter of only relative importance

As someone pointed out recently, the fact I have to repeat
what was recorded, does beckon the question why I spent
£300 on having that recording made in Madrid

Music.

Put wig on.

Upon this table there are two eggs
One egg is real, the other is not
One egg is being serious, being an egg
The other is just joking around, pretending to be an egg
From where you're sitting, can you tell the difference
between the two eggs?
And, is it important that you can tell the difference?

Take wig off.

A few months ago, I'm sitting at my desk, writing
I'm looking at three words – hope, happiness, humanity
I'm writing a collection of short stories under the title *Hope is
a Thin Line*

It includes characters flying happily in hopeful worlds full of
faith in other people
As well as characters drowning in hopeless universes full of
depression and despair. I've been writing non-stop for hours
every day for weeks and months for almost a year. I'm under
pressure

Music.

I have a deadline I really need to meet. I know, if I don't
meet it, I don't get paid, and if I don't get paid, I can't pay
the bills, and if I can't pay the bills I'll be on the streets and
halfway to nowhere. My anxiety is out of control and rising.
I wonder if I'm heading towards a fully-blown nervous
breakdown

My mother calls

Shôn?

Yes, hello Mam, how are you?

I'm fine. I'm just phoning because I forgot to tell you that I
should get my results from the hospital in the next few days.
Eileen said I should let you know

I say
Right. Well, listen, I don't have much on at the moment
– why don't I come up for a few days

You really don't have to do that . . . but it would be nice

I finish the conversation with my mother, pack a bag, go to
the flower shop round the corner and buy some lilies, her
favourite flowers, get in the car and drive to Anglesey where
she has lived her entire life

I know my mother would not have called to share this
information unless she was very anxious
I know my mother is more important than anything I ever
write
I know my mother is not made to last forever

As I drive up north I listen to an interview with Pulitzer
Prize winning American journalist, Isabel Wilkersen

Music.

*There's something about the ways that we are so distant from one
another; too many of us have felt a lack of investment in one another
– we have been programmed to see others as unworthy, undeserving,
distant and we don't feel a connection to one another. These divisions
have a real impact on how we see one another . . .*

I feel like I'm listening to a wise prophet releasing me from a
spell I've been under for decades

I drive onto the island, towards my mother's house
When I arrive, my mother is standing in the doorway
I get out the car and walk towards her

Now this is interesting
She says
What you going to do first – give me a hug or give me the
flowers?

For me, it's obvious. I give her a hug – perhaps the biggest
I've ever given her
I pack a thousand words into the hug
Then Mr Evans, the neighbour, walks out of his house

What a lovely thing to witness
He says
A mother and son embrace

My mother looks at him and says – Is that what it looked like
Mr Evans – the truth is, he was trying to squeeze me to death

Mr Evans laughs and says
Good to see you Shôn. Tell your father I'll be round later to
pick him up for football

I said I would, although my father died over twenty years
ago and he hated football – he was a hard-playing rugby
man. For him, it was a question of masculinity

Mr Evans stands still. It looks like he doesn't know what he's
doing
I say
I think you were heading towards town Mr Evans

Ah! Yes – the newspaper
He says and heads towards town

My mother looks at me a says
Now then Shôn, I'm glad you're here and I enjoyed that
hug, but it was a bit intense. I don't want any big dramas. We
have no idea what the doctor will say, so let's not get carried
away. Let's just stay calm and focus on keeping things
normal

Agreed
I say and fetch my bag from the car

Meanwhile my mother puts the flowers in a vase and puts
the vase on a table in the front room. We meet in the kitchen
for our mandatory cup of tea
Then she asks
I know you've just arrived but do you mind very much
watering the front garden for me please Shôn? It hasn't
rained for days

I say
Of course I can
and go over to the cupboard under the sink and put on a
pair of Marigold gloves

My mother smiles and says
You are a buffoon

There's a hose pipe by the front door, I turn the tap on and
start watering the plants. Then this man walks past – he's
noticeably tall, pale skin, dark hair
I make a bit of a show of the fact that I'm wearing Marigold
gloves
He looks, he doesn't smile, he walks straight on

A few moments later, Mr Evans returns from town. He has a newspaper under his arm. He says

Shôn, I have a gun in the house. Your father gave it to me when he became a pacifist. Do you want it?

No, you keep it Mr Evans
I say

You might need it if you're trying to kill your mother

Really. It's fine Mr Evans. You keep it

Then he asks
As a matter of interest, how long have you been trying to kill your mother for?

I laugh and say
I've only just started actually

Well, good luck with that Shôn
He says
Here's your newspaper

You can have the newspaper
I say

You sure. Very kind. Thank you
He says and disappears into his house

A few moments later, my mother appears at the front door
She looks at the garden and says
Looks better already. Let's go shopping

I put the hose pipe away and we walk into town

Music.

As we walk past the hairdresser's, Eileen steps out
Eileen is my mother's best friend
They've been friends for almost eighty years
They are as connected as the sea is to the land

My mother shouts
Eileen, I hope you didn't pay for that haircut

Eileen laughs and says
I used to love going to the hairdresser's, now it's torture
– sitting in front of a mirror, looking at your neck sagging
like an empty sack. I haven't seen my chin for years – it's
disappeared with my eyesight and half my hearing

Eileen, you are gorgeous and beautiful and everyone loves
you
My mother says

You know what Shôn – your mother is the only reason I'm
still alive. When she goes, I'm going too

A police car drives past us

I knew those two when they were boys terrorising their
mothers to tears
I'm not sure if that makes me feel more safe or more afraid
Eileen says

Eileen is holding onto my elbow
My mother says
Let go of my son Eileen and step away will you – we need to
go shopping
You can pop round later for a cup of tea and a chat if you
really have to

We carry on walking down the High Street
The bins are over-flowing, broken beer bottles on the street,
there are pigeons next to every lamp-post. I notice the sign
above the supermarket door is coming loose from the wall.
It's hanging off a wire, over the entrance. We walk into the
supermarket

Music.

I notice some shelves are empty
I notice others are full
I notice everything is on offer and the lighting at the back of
the shop isn't working properly – it's flickering

We head off down the aisles. I stop by the baked bean tins
and ask
Shall I get some beans Mam

She says
Yes, of course

I grab a pack of four tins and put them in the trolley. I
pause, look at my mother, then I grab another pack of four
and put them in the trolley. I look at my mother again. She's
smiling. Then I grab four more packs of four and put them
in the trolley. I look at my mother. She's almost laughing. I
grab another four packs of four and then another pack of
four. I look at the thirty-two tins of beans I've put in the
trolley, then I look at my mother. She's very very close to
laughing. I ask

D'you think that's enough Mam, or shall I put a few more in?

My mother laughs and says
I can't believe I gave birth to such a ginormous buffoon

The two of us stand there by the trolley full of beans, laughing
The two of us have always enjoyed joking around

Music.

One of the highlights of our joking around happened in the
kitchen when I was eight. My mother cracked an egg on my
forehead while I helped her make pancakes. While I held
the bowl, full of mixture, she nonchalantly cracked an egg
on my forehead and laughed as the egg yoke dripped down
my face. Then she took the bowl off me and let me crack an
egg on her head too. I laughed so hard it changed my shape
and made me love laughter forever

So, the two of us are standing there in the supermarket aisle
by the trolley full of tins of beans, laughing. Then the man I
saw earlier – the one who didn't react to my Marigold gloves
– tall, pale skin, dark hair – comes up to me and asks
What's so funny about loading up your trolley with tins of
baked beans?

I say
Ermm, well it's funny I suppose because . . . I put in far
more than we actually need

Right

Ermm . . . it's like – say it's cold and I'm standing outside
with a jumper on, then I go, 'Brrrr, it's cold', and I go into
the house and come back out with ten jumpers on . . .

Right

Well, it's the same principle . . . you know . . . it's
exaggeration . . . listen . . . it's alright, it's OK, I'm just joking
around with my mother – we're just having a bit of fun

Then he says
You've come to the supermarket for fun? You go to a
supermarket for shopping. You go to a play centre for fun.
What d'you think would happen if everybody came to the
supermarket for fun?

So, of course I say
Then the play centre would be empty

What?

Well, I mean, if everyone came here to have fun, the play
centre would be empty

Are you taking the piss mate?

No

D'you want me to punch you?

No

I'm just joking around. I wouldn't punch you. You're tiny

And then my mother comes up to us and says
C'mon Shôn. Let's carry on with the shopping

Then the man says
Is this your mother . . . you've come shopping with your

mother. You're a Mummy's Boy. Oh! You're a little Mummy's Boy! Then he laughs. He finds that really funny. He laughs a lot and heads out of the supermarket

My mother says
You need to ignore people like that. Don't let them get their hooks into you

Then I put the tins from the trolley back on the shelf and we walk around the supermarket filling the trolley with things we actually need

We push the trolley to the checkout just before the wheels stop turning completely
Elen sits there – we were in the same class at primary school
Causing trouble again are you
She says
I laugh and say
Who the hell was that?

I have no idea who he is, but he knows exactly who you are
Shôn – a Mummy's Boy

Glad to see you've still got your sense of humour Elen
I say

Then Elen says to me
I suppose it's OK that you come in here and joke around, but it took me a long time this morning to load the shelves and I noticed that when you put those beans back, you didn't put them back properly

I turn round to look at the shelf of baked beans. They look untidy, but I can't figure out why. I say to Elen
I suppose it's because I don't have the same shelf-stacking skills as you've got

The same what?

The same shelf-staking skills

That's right Shôn, I've got shelf-stacking skills. When I started working here I didn't have shelf-stacking skills. I

acquired my shelf-stacking skills on the job. And now I've
got shelf-stacking skills I can tell you the reason they don't
look right is because all the labels aren't facing the same way

Clever
I say

Clever. That's right Shôn, you have to be clever to work here

Elen scans the items and packs the bags as she goes, then
she says
£55.74p please

I say
The food in here is overpriced. I refuse to pay the
extortionate amount you're charging. You can keep your
shopping, we're going elsewhere

Elen says
You might think that's funny Shôn, but that is the reaction I
get from some people. People round here are on the brink

You're right
I say
The price of food isn't funny

Damn right it's not funny. People in power in this country
are trying to starve us lot. We used to be useful to them when
they needed us for cannon fodder. Now they've invented
drones, we've become completely useless

My mother butts in and says
I think I'll pay for this before the bleakness blinds me
and gets her cash card out and goes to tap the machine

I take out my cash card and say
I'll pay

No, I'll pay
My mother says

No. I'll pay
I say and tap my card on the machine

Then my mother asks
Did you check the eggs?

And I say
No, but I'm sure they're fine

You should always check the eggs
She says

I repeat
I'm sure they're fine

You should check them
She says

I insist
I'm sure they're fine. Anyway, we've paid for them already

Elen says
I'll check the eggs for you Mummy's Boy

No Elen
I say
It's fine, seriously, you don't need to check them, really,
thank you

Come on
She says
It'll take less than a second

I say
No, seriously, it's fine

I put my hand on the bag. She puts her hand on the bag at
the same time
I pull the bag towards me
Then she holds her finger and goes
Ow!

Then she looks at her finger and says
You split my fingernail

Now, when I look back on that moment, I know that all I
should have done was say
I'm sorry, are you OK?

But I don't do that. Probably because I'm wound up

I don't say anything. I take the bag. I walk past the baked
beans. I get to the door
I stand in the doorway. And I remember a little pigeon
looking at me. Judging me

I look at Elen and my mother

Music.

Elen is holding her finger
My mother must have simply said goodbye to Elen
She walks towards me. She stops by the baked beans and
puts the tins right – you know, so the labels are all facing the
same way

When I look back on it, of course, I know, I should have
gone to help my mother. But I don't. I don't know why, but
I don't

And then my mother walks towards me and I know exactly
what she wants to say to me, because it's written all over
her face

Go to your room and don't come out until you've learnt how
to behave

As we walk back home I'm a prisoner inside my own Shame
Prison
I feel like the silence between us is going to break my bones
I notice that next to the hairdresser's there's a funeral
parlour
And that the window sill is caked in pigeon shit

When we get to the front door of my mother's house, my
mother looks at me and says
I just don't understand why you didn't check the eggs Shôn

I put the shopping bag down. I admit I felt a bit irritated.
I reach into the bag and wrestle out the box of eggs. I say
If I open this box and find that not a single egg is cracked,
what are the consequences?

My mother says
You know what the consequences are

Really
I say

I open the box and look at the eggs. I check them and
double check them
I pass the box to my mother, she inspects them then looks at
me and says
Please crack an egg upon my forehead

I take an egg out of the box, my mother presents her
forehead and stands still
I place my left hand behind her head, and cradle it in my
palm
I hold an egg in my right hand
She's smiling. I'm smiling

Do what I say Shôn
She says
Crack it on my head

Music.

I crack the egg on her forehead
I feel her head jolt back into my left hand
The yoke drips down her face
My mother bursts out laughing
She's laughing so hard, it looks like she's crying
She's laughing so hard, it looks like she's crying

Then we notice Mr Evans, the neighbour
He's looking at us
We look at him. He looks back at us
He looks really confused

I wave at him. He does not wave back
He walks off into town

My mother says, with egg yoke on her face
Come on Shôn, let's go in

I open the door and we walk into the house and go through
to the kitchen
I put the bag on the kitchen counter and start unpacking the
produce, putting things where they should be, on shelves
and suchlike, then I turn and see my mother standing,
looking at me, holding an egg. She says
Now it's my turn

Music.

I present my forehead to my mother, I stand still and she
cracks an egg on my forehead
We both stand in the kitchen with egg yoke dripping down
our faces, laughing
I'm eight years old again, in the kitchen, making pancakes

We clean the egg off our faces, then my mother asks
Shôn, do you mind going upstairs to the attic – I'm sure
your father's binoculars are up there and they'll be more
useful down here

Mam
I say
I don't mind doing that for £50

I was going to offer you £100
She says

I say
I'm more than happy to do it for £100. Thank you very
much

I go upstairs, open the hatch in the ceiling, pull the ladder
down and climb into the attic. It's almost empty. I panic.
She's cleared the bloody attic. She knows she's going to die

Music.

There are only two boxes up there. One box is marked spare pillows and blankets, the other is marked bits'n'bobs. I open the one marked bits'n'bobs. I see my father's binoculars and a shoe box. I take them both out. I sit under the Velux window and open the shoe box. Inside the shoe box is every letter and postcard I've ever written to my mother. I read a postcard I sent in 1987. I'm eighteen years old. It's from a Greek island. It has a black and white photograph of a donkey on the front of it

I've written
Dear Mam,
Thanks for bringing me up. I'm pleased to let you know that your parenting job is now over. On the whole, as a mother, you were pretty disappointing.
Love,
Shôn

I climb back down with my father's binoculars and the shoe box
I find my mother in the front room. She's looking at the lilies
She says
Funny gift flowers – essentially, you put them in a vase and watch them die

I say
That's definitely one way of looking at it. It's all very well organised up there Mam

Yes, I've given what I can to charity and chucked the rest. I wanted it all sorted so there's nothing for you to clear away after I've gone

She sees the shoe box

I was hoping you'd find that box after I've died. I've snuck a surprise letter in there for you from beyond the grave. My very last bit of joking around with you

Then she claps her hands and says
You know what Shôn, I think there's a good chance that
dying is going to be brilliant

Then she stands up and says
Let me show you my new favourite thing – sit in the comfy
chair by the window with your father's binoculars

The window overlooks the Menai Strait and the Snowdonia
Mountain Range
She goes to the stereo system she got for Christmas and puts
some music on

Music.

Watch the birds and imagine they are dancing to the music
you can hear

I follow her instructions
The Menai Strait becomes a stage and the mountains
become a backdrop

As if from nowhere, birds appear, one after another
Flying alone, in pairs and threes
They twist and turn in and out of each other
Then dive towards the water and skim the surface
Before flying back upwards
They stop in mid air, undoing dizziness
Then circle round and go again
Diving swooping skimming
Twisting and turning
More birds appear
Flying upwards
Lifting each other higher
Disappearing into the sun
Reappearing above the mountains
Daring to dive faster
Making nonsense out of fireworks
Weaving magic as they fly

There's a knock on the door. I'm back in the house
I'll get it
I say

It's Eileen. It's windy outside but her hair is perfectly still

I'm disappointed in you Shôn
She says and walks past me into the front room

My mother gets up from her chair
What's wrong Eileen?

Mr Evans said you were crying. He said Shôn smashed an
egg on your head

We were joking around Eileen. Come and sit down. You
don't want to listen to what Mr Evans says. The other day he
said he saw a humpback whale rise up out of the Menai
Strait

She passes Eileen my father's binoculars
Take a seat and make yourself comfortable – we can both
enjoy watching the birds at the same time

Shall I make a pot of tea
I ask

No
my mother says
Bring the gin and two glasses

An hour later I'm walking Eileen home
She's holding my elbow and she says to me
If it wasn't for your mother I don't know what I'd do. I've
run out of hope. Happiness is a song playing in the distance.
This town is drowning and it's dragging me with it. I'm
stuck here. The buses hardly ever turn up. There's no cash
point – the bank has literally taken all their money away. The
primary school has closed. People can't afford children.
People drink like there's no tomorrow. Everyone living off
yesterday. Not a dentist in sight. Teeth dropping out of faces
like rainfall. I sit at home in the cold and dark knowing that

in other parts of the world bombs drop on innocent people, as if that should make me feel lucky. Well I do not feel lucky. I feel angry. I'm more angry now than I've ever been in my entire life. I thought by this age, I'd be looked after. Instead, I get the front row seat, to watch the pigeons shit everywhere. This town is being smothered in excrement. Sometimes I go to bed and I lie there and I think, I hope I don't wake up in the morning. Oh! Here we are. Thank you for walking me home and protecting me from the pigeons. That was very nice of you. Very nice indeed. Now, listen Shôn, your job right now is to make sure your mother leaves here in the best way possible. It's the biggest job of your life. Don't mess it up, otherwise it'll haunt you forever. Your mother will only die once

She puts her key in the front door and disappears

I stand on her doorstep under the big dark night sky, realising that I have absolutely no idea what it's like to be an old person living in this world

I find myself walking back through town. The street lights come on. One in three don't work. I notice a sign on the window of the funeral parlour;
Two for the price of one. Enquire within.
Now that's funny, I think to myself

I see Elen walking towards me. She has her eight-year-old grandson with her. As she gets closer, I see she has a plaster on her finger. As soon as she gets to me she says
Bloody hell Shôn, what the hell is going on! People have been coming in and out of the shop all afternoon talking about it. Why did you smash an egg on your mother's face. What on earth were you thinking?

While she's talking, her grandson, Rhys, is kicking my ankle. I look at him

Elen says
That's right Rhys, give him a good kicking

Rhys looks at me, then kicks me really hard
I look at Elen. Then I look at him and say
I don't think you should kick me

Fuck you
He says
You shouldn't crack eggs on your mam's face

I look at Elen.
That's right Rhys, you tell him
She says

Then, eight-year-old Rhys looks at me and says

Music.

Fuck you, asshole. You're an absolute mother fuckin' idiot
and you know it – shit face tosser

I look at Elen. She's smiling

He takes out three cigarettes, puts them all in his mouth and
lights them
He stands there smoking, kicking me, then he jumps up on
the bin, grabs the lamp-post, climbs up it then jumps back
down onto the bin. The bin collapses. There's litter all over
the street. He kicks me again. I look at Elen. She's still
smiling. He takes ketamine out of his jacket, snorts it, grabs a
pigeon, wrings the pigeon's neck and pulls its head off and
sucks blood from its body and kicks me. He takes his phone
out and starts swiping through porn. I look at him and he
kicks me really hard, again

Elen laughs out loud
Nice one Rhys
She says
And the two of them walk off

I'm left standing there, watching at least nine pigeons
pecking away at the end of a battered sausage. All I want to
do is get back to my mother's house. I start walking. I walk
faster. My fast walk turns into a run. I sprint round the

corner and see the man from the supermarket standing on
Mr Evans's doorstep talking to him. Mr Evans sees me and
closes the door. The man from the supermarket stares at me.
I ignore him and focus on my mother's front door. As I open
the door I can't help glancing at him quickly

Music.

I step inside the house. He's freaked me out. I can feel the
adrenaline kick in.

Then I hear my mother's voice from upstairs
Hello. Is that Shôn, or is it Billy the Burglar?

Of course, I decide to join in. I say
It's me. Billy the Burglar

Oh Billy! Please don't steal the lovely lilies my son bought
for me

I'm sorry but they're what attracted me in here

Please Billy. Take the vase

OK. I'll just take the vase

Listen Billy, I just want to tell Shôn that I'm off to bed and
thank you for walking Eileen home
She says
She needs all the support she can get. Good night

I shout good night up the stairs and I stand by the door
knowing that there's no way I'll fall asleep in the state I'm in.
I walk into the front room, grab a book from the bookshelf
– *Legends from the Thirteenth Century* – draw the curtains
closed and turn the reading lamp on. I stay up reading the
Welsh legend of Gelert the Dog. It's a simple story. It goes
like this

Music.

Llewlyn, the Prince of North Wales, leaves his baby son
under the watchful eye of his beloved dog, Gelert, while he
goes hunting. When he returns, he goes straight to his baby

son's cot. His son isn't there. He panics. He sees his beloved dog, Gelert, covered in blood. He looks at the empty cot. He looks at Gelert. He takes out his sword and kills the dog he loves. At the exact same moment, he hears the sound of a baby crying. He runs out into the yard. He sees a wolf lying in a pool of blood. He hears the baby cry again. He finds his son alive and well, hidden under a blanket. He lifts his baby up to his chest and looks at his dead dog. It is said that the Prince never smiled again

The next day when I wake up I find a note in the kitchen Such beautiful light this morning I've gone down to the headland

I walk into town. I want to apologise to Elen for snatching the bag off her

I notice there are at least fifteen pigeons outside the funeral parlour and that the two-for-one offer is still there in the window. As I approach the supermarket, I notice how thin the wire is, holding the sign above the door. I walk in

The lights are flickering
I notice the baked bean tins are perfectly arranged, all the labels facing the same way
I walk to the checkout, looking for Elen. She's not there
I see a pile of leaflets on the counter
There's a photograph of me on the front of the leaflet
There's a photograph of me on the front of the leaflet, under two words – Moral Crisis
I pick up the leaflet. On the other side I read,
Middle aged man smashes egg on elderly mother's face
Is our community happy to live beside this sort of behaviour?

The man appears
He says
Are you here to play with the baked bean tins again Shôn

I say
If you're in any way responsible for these leaflets, I'm sure the police will have something to say about them

You want to bring the police into this Shôn?

You and I know that the source of your information is an old man called Mr Evans.
An old man who recently claimed to have seen a humpbacked whale rise up out of the Menai Strait

Then I add, very assertively. Probably over-assertively
And, I'm not happy with you calling me by my first name, thank you very much

He steps towards me
Mr Evans saw your mother crying as a consequence of you smashing an egg in her face Shôn

I make a crystal clear statement of fact
She was not crying. She was laughing

Of course you'd say that. You won't get away with your behaviour. We're onto you Shôn

I have no idea what to say next.
Suddenly, my hands pick up all the leaflets on the counter

One leaflet per person
The man says

I say very loudly
Where on the leaflet does it say that?

Elen appears. I notice she has a bandage on her hand

Holding the leaflet up I say
This can't be allowed, surely . . . I mean . . . what are these leaflets doing on your counter?

That man insisted I leave them here on the counter. He said the leaflets enabled freedom of information to circulate around the town

But Elen . . .
I say

Don't you but Elen me Mummy's Boy
She says
I'm not having your buts. Your mother told you to check the
eggs. You refused to check them. I'm a mother too. If my
son behaved like you, I'd be disappointed. You were rude to
your mother – you dismissed her. I liked you as a boy Shôn,
but I do not like you as an adult. You are an arrogant little
man. If the world wasn't run by arrogant little men like you
I wouldn't be here overworked and underpaid in a shop
with a flickering light that does my head in

I walk towards the door. The man shouts
Who in their right mind would take fifty leaflets

I turn around and shout
Who in their right mind would let an eight-year-old boy kick
a grown man in the street

I carry on walking towards the door and as I walk through
it, the sign falls right in front of me. I think I'm going to shit
my pants. I step over the sign and carry on walking

The man shouts after me
No one in their right mind would take fifty leaflets

As I walk past the funeral parlour, I see a poster next to their
two-for-one offer
It's a wanted poster with my face on it

I see Mr Evans across the road. He's feeding the pigeons
bread. As I walk over to him, he sees me and scuttles away.
I'm surrounded by pigeons in the middle of a feeding frenzy

I watch Mr Evans disappear round the corner

When I get home, I walk straight through the house, into
the kitchen
I put the leaflets on the table and look at them more closely
I try to calm down. I need to be methodical. Analytical.

Forensic
I read
This man's egg-cracking behaviour is just the tip of the
ice-berg – imagine what else he does to her behind closed
doors
I decide I can't get drawn into this madness
I pick up the leaflets, dump them in the bin and put the
kettle on

There's a knock on the door

The man from the supermarket is standing there with three
other people I've never seen before. He says
We're here to get the leaflets you stole from the supermarket

A woman with long hair and a smart jacket steps forward
and says
You cracked an egg on your mother's forehead. That's evil.
You are evil. You're going to pay for what you've done.
You're going to wish you were never born

I almost laugh. I mean, it's so over the top
I notice one of the group is filming everything on his phone
I feel like I'm standing on the set of a horror film

I ask
Can you tell me who you are please. It's not clear on the
leaflets you produced who you are or who you represent

The woman says
Bring your mother here. Bring her to the door

I say
She's not here

That's convenient
She says, making a huge theatrical gesture
Let me go inside to check

I say
No. You are not coming into my house

It's not your house. It's your mother's house. Stand aside,
I'm coming in

The tall pale man from the supermarket puts his arm on her
shoulder and says
Let's leave it there for today Janet
He looks at me and says
I'll invoice you for the leaflets you stole Shôn

The four of them walk away

I go back to the kitchen. By now, the kettle's boiled
It takes all my concentration to make a simple cup of tea
Their venom has inflamed my neural pathways and dragged
me to the dark recesses of my mind where great acts of
violence are perpetrated

Some friends tell me they think that line is over-written, but
I've decided to leave it in

My mother's note is still on the table
I'm here for her, I remind myself. I'm here for her
I look at my mother's handwriting. I panic

Music.

I see her sitting in the kitchen, writing the note. I see her
throwing herself off the headland, into the sea. I see her
drowning. I see her dead body being dragged out of the sea.
I see Eileen weeping. Then I hear my mother walk in
through the front door

She's alive. She's alive. She walks into the kitchen. I get up
out of my chair and give her an enormous hug

I've had the most wonderful walk around the headland
She says
Unfortunately I did not see a humpbacked whale rise up out
of the Strait, but I did find the perfect spot to be buried. A
spot where all the beauty of all the world hit me all at once

Then she says very gently
I've seen the wanted posters. I know about the leaflets. I've

spoken to Elen and I've spoken to the police. They say they are going to send a community officer round to talk to you. Don't you worry about all this Shôn

I'm sorry Mam, I have no idea why I didn't check the eggs. I'm an absolute buffoon

Then my mother looks at me, smiles and says
You know what – knowing you're a buffoon is half the battle. The worst thing about all this is that wanted poster. I mean, where did they get that photograph? It's the worst haircut you've ever had

When the community officer comes round, the two of us sit in the kitchen
My mother sits in the front room, watching the birds

I don't know how this situation translates into your lives, but for me, when the community officer walks into the house, wearing her police uniform, it really unnerved me. I suppose it's the association that the uniform has with crime. I suppose it was because it hit me that this situation was becoming a legal matter. It definitely didn't make me feel safe

I stood in the kitchen filling the kettle with water while the community officer watched

That's a lot of water you put in the kettle
She says

I don't know how to respond, so I say
I think it holds a litre

She asks
Before we begin do you have any questions?

I say
Yes, d'you take milk and sugar in your tea?

She says
I don't mean questions about how I take my tea

She's completely straight faced. It definitely doesn't feel like the best start I've ever made to a conversation

She says
So that you know, I'm happy for you to call me Carol. Would you like me to call you Shôn?

And I say
No. I'd like you to call me Peter

Peter?

Yes, Peter

OK. Is that your middle name?

No

Is it your friend's name?

No. I just made it up. On the spot. I'm sorry. I was just joking around

Joking around. OK. I'm going to be upfront with you, in the world I belong to, in the echo-chamber that I'm part of, I don't think a middle-aged man cracking an egg on his elderly mother's head is normal behaviour

I understand Carol, but the two of us have a very particular relationship. We were just joking around. We were having fun

Yes, but these people don't see it as fun, they see it as being wrong

No, they don't see it as being wrong, Carol. They see it as being
(*Shouts.*) You cracked an egg on your mother's head, that's evil
I would be half as concerned as I am if they saw it as being wrong
The fact they see it as being evil is really concerning
I can get my head around you saying it's not normal behaviour.

I can even get my head around people saying it's wrong.
But I can't get my head around people saying it's evil

I pour the water from the kettle into a tea pot and put a cup
on the table in front of her

I don't want any tea thank you Shôn. I don't drink on duty
She says and pushes the cup to one side. Completely straight
faced. Then she asks
Had you argued with your mother earlier in the day?

No Carol

Ah! The woman at the checkout told us that you and your
mother argued about checking the eggs

It wasn't an argument. We had a disagreement at best

A disagreement

Yes. Not an argument

And the woman at the checkout – her finger was damaged in
a physical altercation with you

It wasn't a physical altercation, it was a . . . it was a . . . I don't
know how I'd describe it . . .

Well, however we describe it, the fact is, it resulted in Elen's
finger being damaged

Elen did not damage her finger – she split her fingernail.
This feels like I'm being interrogated. And I have no idea
why you would watch me prepare a cup of tea for you and
then tell me you don't want one

You're angry

I'm struggling to make sense of what's going on

Let me explain to you what's happening here. You assumed
I wanted tea. You're assumption was wrong. In fact, your
assumption was evil

I look at Carol. She looks back at me. Straight faced. Then she winks

I laugh. I say
Seriously, I feel like I'm losing it

She says, sympathetically
That's normal. You are the victim of an attack

I suppose I am
I say

What about your mother?

She's doing OK

Are you sure she's OK. I mean, you smashed an egg in her face

I did not smash an egg in her face. I cracked an egg on her forehead. There's a very big difference. When I asked you, do you take milk and sugar in your tea, you didn't say, I don't want tea, so, of course I assumed you wanted tea. You had an opportunity right there to say, I don't want tea. You didn't take the opportunity, so it was normal that I assumed you wanted tea. D'you see. My mother is in the front room. We can go through there now and she can tell you what happened herself

We don't need to do that. She's already given her statement at the police station. But, if we were to go through to the front room would you come with me?

Probably. Yes

And what about Peter? Would he come too? Or would he stay here?

It's difficult all this joking around. What I'm getting here is that you have anger management issues. Just so you know, the woman at the checkout is exploring the possibilities of opening an investigation into what you did to her in the supermarket

You're telling me that Elen is . . . hang on! Big hairy bollocks
– you're joking. This is a joke!

Carol has a straight face. I say
Carol, if you're joking, please wink

Carol does not wink. She stands up
I do not need the image of big hairy bollocks in my mind
thank you very much. The use of that imagery is offensive.
We will conclude this meeting here. I'd prefer if you didn't
call me Carol from this point on. For your information, this
meeting has been recorded. I'll see myself out

I sit in the kitchen looking at the tea I made for Carol.
Why did I say, big hairy bollocks
It's not as if it's one of my stock phrases
I actually can't remember the last time I said 'big hairy
bollocks'
Then my mind fills with them. First I see one big hairy
bollock appear in the tea cup – it floats to the surface, then it
climbs out of the tea cup and rolls around the table and falls
onto the kitchen floor. As the big hairy bollock rolls around
the kitchen floor, it gets bigger and bigger until it explodes
into hundreds of smaller hairy bollocks. Then these smaller
hairy bollocks float about in the kitchen. One lands on a
spoon, one lands on the kettle, then my mother appears

Did you have a good chat with Carol?

I clear my mind of bollocks

Yes
I say
I had a good chat with Carol. It was very useful. Thank you
for asking her to come round

Then I say
Mam, listen, I'm really sorry I didn't check the eggs in the
supermarket. It was rude not to

She looks at me and says
Well Shôn, I'm really very sorry but I can't forgive you for
that. It's something I will take with me to my grave

Then she says
On that subject, I've decided for definite – I want to be
buried. Not cremated. And, so that you know, Eileen is going
to do her very best to die at the same time as I do so we can
get that two-for-one deal that the funeral parlour is offering

I say
Mam, I don't want you to die

Music.

Death is when life becomes most real
It's when reality becomes completely inescapable

She looks at me and says
Listen Shôn, not even Houdini could escape this one. I'd
love to stay and chat, but right now I need to go to see Eileen
– she's having a crisis about her hair

My mother puts her overcoat on and leaves the house

I'm left there with this feeling. I think to myself, this is
ridiculous to feel this way now. And so I get the shoe box
– you know – the one I found in the attic. I put the shoe box
on the table

Music.

I take all the letters out
I see my mother's handwriting on the front of an envelope
It simply says
For Shôn
I get a knife from the drawer and open the envelope very
carefully
Inside is a postcard
On the front of the postcard is a black and white photograph
of a donkey
On the back she's written

Dear Shôn
I hope you enjoy reading these words from me, beyond the grave.
I thought I'd tell you straight – throughout my entire life, as a son, you were always a huge disappointment to me.
Love,
Mam

And then the phone rings. I answer it
Are you Shôn?
A voice asks
Yes I am
I say
Would you like to comment on the article online

I put the phone down and type my name into Google
A newspaper article appears
The same picture of my face that they used for the wanted poster comes up under the headline – Violent Misogynist
I read below the headline
Welsh Island Terror Alert – Middle-aged man caught smashing eggs on elderly
I scroll down
In capital letters I find the question
DO YOU FIND HIS BEHAVIOUR OUTRAGEOUS?
It has a yes and a no button next to the question
Within one minute the number of yeses goes up from thirty-seven to fifty-nine to108 to 1,803 to – I am not joking – 7,641
Comments below the article start to appear, and they come from all over the world
Big John, Texas – Drown him in egg yoke
Su Will Sue, Singapore – Scramble his head until he cries like a baby
I'm almost laughing because they're sort of funny
Then this anonymous comment appears
Another arsehole that needs killing

Music.

There's a knock on the door
The two policemen that I saw driving past the other day
when I was with Eileen outside the hairdresser's are
standing there

Shôn, sorry, Mr Dale-Jones, me, PC Roberts and PC Pissy
Pants here need to talk to you. Can we come inside

They step into the house

Is that as photograph of your mother?
PC Roberts asks

Yes
I say
It's a photo of her on her wedding day

Very nice
He says

We walk into the kitchen

No microwave I see. I'm sorry, we're going to have to arrest
you for that. But seriously, the reason we're here is because
Carol, the community officer, came round, interviews you,
recorded everything, we've listened to the recording and
she, Carol, has made a formal complaint. But don't worry,
she and the other women on the force are all up to it at the
minute, you know, it's the environment we're in. Everyone
jumping on the band wagon. We're taking it with a pinch of
salt but it does mean that you need to take your trousers
down

Sorry

Take your trousers down and show us your big hairy
bollocks

Music.

Don't panic Shôn – we're just joking around
We don't want to see your big hairy bollocks
When we were boys we terrorised our mothers to tears

You don't need to worry about the leaflets and wanted posters and all that
Us mother-hating children need to stick together

I don't hate my mother, I love her
I say

I'm not sure if they hear me. They don't react. They walk out of the house

I walk out of the house after them. They get in their car
I shout
I don't hate my mother, I love her

They drive off

Then, from the corner they drive round, the man from the supermarket appears
He appears with over thirty people following him
Then two mini-buses park outside the house
At least twenty people get out carrying banners
I'm not joking, one reads
DO NOT LET EGG-CRACKER EGGSIST ON THIS ISLAND

I look at the man from the supermarket and say
What words can I use to make you understand that what you are doing here is wrong, if not evil

Janet – the woman with the long hair and smart jacket
– steps forward and says
If I had it my way, I'd get a chainsaw and chop your hands off so you couldn't ever crack an egg again. Then I'd chop your arms and legs off and make you eat them

I look at the man from the supermarket and say
You have to put a stop to this. I mean, this is so out of proportion

This is all happening because of you Shôn
He says

I say
OK, I apologise for cracking the egg on my mother's head

Apology insincere. Apology not accepted

The crowd are standing there chanting, Out Out Out
They're hurling abuse at me
I have no option. I retreat into the house. I close the front
door then I hear a knock on the back door. I walk through
the corridor to the kitchen. I look through the kitchen
window and I see Mr Evans. I open the door. He has a gun
in his hand

This is your father's gun. You look like you might need it
He says

I look at the gun. I look at Mr Evans. Then I say
No Mr Evans, I don't need a gun. And, to be honest, I do
not need you telling people you saw my mother crying when
she was laughing. You need to learn the difference between
people being serious and people joking around

And he says
I do know the difference. When that woman was going on
about chopping your hands off, she was joking around

I look at him and say
No Mr Evans, she was being serious. And, I'll tell you what
– when they chop my hands off, I'll post them through your
letterbox, so that you know

Mr Evans looks at me and says
You're joking around. And I know you're joking around
because you would struggle to pick up your hands if they'd
already chopped them off

Then I say
Mr Evans, I'm being serious, the humpbacked whale you
saw rise up out of the Menai Strait is going to swim on shore
and find you. It's going to drag you into the water and
drown you

Mr Evans looks right at me and says
That's not going to happen because I'm going to shoot
myself

Then he lifts the gun to his head
I push him with my left hand and grab the gun with my
right
He's lying flat on the ground. I'm standing over him with
the gun
I'm like Llewelyn, the Prince of North Wales, standing over
his beloved dog, Gelert

I was just joking around
He says

Mr Evans, you do not joke around with a gun. Like you do
not joke around about the price of food

I offer him my hand
Come on Mr Evans, let's get you back up on your feet

Your father was a pacifist. He'd be ashamed of you

Mr Evans disappears back into his house

I can hear the crowd outside chanting, Out Out Out
I can hear them hurling abuse
Then I think to myself
Fuck this

Music.

I open the front door and I look at the crowd and I shout
You lot are aliens. Why don't you fuck off back to outer space
where you come from. If you don't leave here in less than
one minute I swear I will kill one of you
Then I see Elen and Rhys passing boxes of eggs to people in
the crowd
An egg flies past my head and hits the door behind me
Then one hits my knee, my chest, my shoulder, my arm, my
thigh
Eggs explode all over me – I'm dripping in egg yoke

Egg yoke is seeping into my mouth and going up my
nostrils. I can't breathe
Then I see little eight-year-old Rhys standing right in front
of me with an egg
He pulls his arm back and throws an egg from point blank
range into my hairy bollocks. I grab him and I shout
Rhys you're a stupid little fascist cunt

Music cuts.

The crowd stop throwing eggs
Elen looks at me and says
Are you sure you want to call an eight-year-old child a stupid
little fascist cunt
And I say
Yes I fuckin' am

Music.

I see the hose pipe. I see the tap
I turn the tap on and point the hose pipe at the crowd
The water shoots out like a line of steel
Someone shouts
He's spraying acid
People start screaming, tearing their clothes off
Seriously. Who are these people
Then two of them, using their banners like shields, they
push me down to the ground
Now there are ten of them on me
There's a hand over my nostrils
They push the tap into my mouth
Janet appears, she's screaming
Turn the tap on full. Fill him up with water. Cleanse him.
He's evil. Cleanse him
I can feel my body bloating to twice its size
I'm sure I'm going to die like a bloated chicken

Music builds to a crescendo, then cuts.

Just ignore them
My mother says
Don't let them get their hooks into you

Eileen agrees. She says the same thing

Let's go and watch the birds
My mother says

We go through to the front room. The lilies sit on a small table.

She goes over to the stereo she got for Christmas and puts some music on

Music.

Eileen has brought her own set of binoculars. The three of us sit together

We sit overlooking the Menai Strait and the Snowndonia Mountain Range.

We watch the birds dive, swoop and skim the surface of the water

There's a loud knock on the door

Ignore it
My mother says

They knock again
Ignore it. They'll go away

They knock again. Harder
Then again. Harder
Then there's a knock on the back door
They're knocking on both the front door and the back door

My mother says
Shôn, trust me, they will go away eventually

We carry on watching the birds

The knocking gets louder and louder
They start knocking on the windows
The knocking doesn't stop

My mother gets up and says
Come on, let's go upstairs and climb onto the roof. We can
watch the birds from there

We climb into the attic and through the Velux window

I take the box marked pillows and blankets

My mother and Eileen sit on pillows on the roof wrapped in
blankets looking up at the sky
The sky is falling into sunset
The birds are flying in perfect unison
The sky is slowly turning pink
The birds twist and turn
Using deeply embedded thermal mapping systems to
calculate where each other are in space – the birds fly in lines
and circles, criss-crossing each other at high speed – it's an
incredible thing these little birds can do

I watch my mother and Eileen watching the birds
The birds swoop closer and closer to the roof

My mother turns to me and says
Shôn, are you ready for this

Then, as the birds swoop towards the roof, my mother and
Eileen stand up, spread their arms, making their blankets
look like wings, lean forward and let themselves go with the
birds

They fly upwards towards the sun

I watch as they fly into the sunlight and disappear for a
moment

I look over the edge of the roof
The mob are all looking up at the sky, they're watching the
birds

Then, as the birds swoop down again, my mother flies past
Her arms are still stretched out, holding the blanket. Her
eyes are shining
She shouts
I told you I thought dying was going to be brilliant

She flies upwards, twisting and turning as she rises, flying
faster and higher, weaving between all the other birds, until
she disappears into the light

I'm left looking at the sky

The sky turns from pink to red to orange

I don't want to stop looking at the sky

It has been a big pleasure being here tonight
And of course that is what I say at the end of this show every
time I perform it
But being here with you tonight makes me feel like I'd say it
Even if I hadn't planned to
Thanks for coming
Good night